D0688267

DATE DUE

ASTORIA PUBLIC LIBRARY
450 10th Street
Astoria, OR 97103

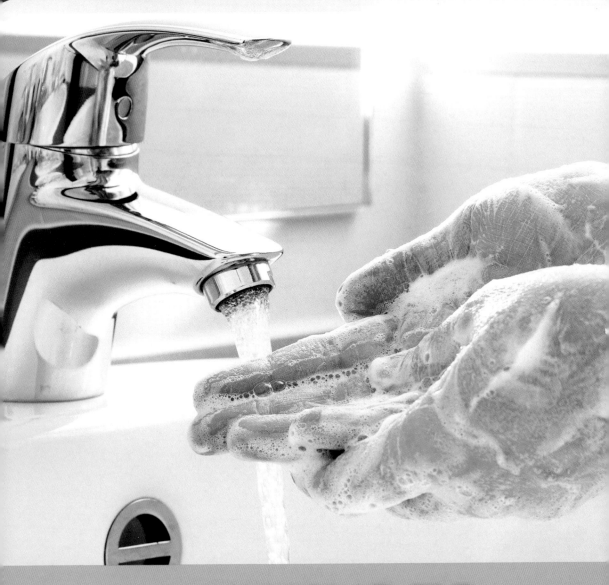

12 WAYS TO
PREVENT DISEASE

by Melissa Abramovitz

12 STORY
LIBRARY

www.12StoryLibrary.com

Copyright © 2017 by Peterson Publishing Company, North Mankato, MN 56003. All rights reserved. No part of this book may be reproduced or utilized in any form or by any means without written permission from the publisher.

12-Story Library is an imprint of Peterson Publishing Company and Press Room Editions.

Produced for 12-Story Library by Red Line Editorial

Photographs ©: Alexander Raths/Shutterstock Images, cover, 1; Adisa/Shutterstock Images, 4; Lissandra Melo/Shutterstock Images, 5; Rob Marmion/Shutterstock Images, 6; pathdoc/Shutterstock Images, 7; bitt24/Shutterstock Images, 8; Evikka/Shutterstock Images, 9; karelnoppe/iStockphoto, 10; Tom Wang/Shutterstock Images, 11; StepanPopov/Shutterstock Images, 12; kitty/Shutterstock Images, 13; Fotokostic/Shutterstock Images, 14; Paolo Bona/Shutterstock Images, 15; Margoe Edwards/Shutterstock Images, 16; Josh Rinehults/iStockphoto, 17, 29; Rob Byron/Shutterstock Images, 18; EdStock/iStockphoto, 19; Juanmonino/iStockphoto, 20; junpinzon/Shutterstock Images, 21; Kalcutta/Shutterstock Images, 22; pbombaert/Shutterstock Images, 23; AnastasiaKopa/Shutterstock Images, 24; spass/Shutterstock Images, 25; Blend Images/Shutterstock Images, 26; kurhan/Shutterstock Images, 27

Library of Congress Cataloging-in-Publication Data
Cataloging-in-publication information is on file with the Library of Congress.
978-1-63235-370-2 (hardcover)
978-1-63235-388-7 (paperback)
978-1-62143-512-9 (hosted ebook)

Printed in the United States of America
Mankato, MN
May, 2016

Access free, up-to-date content on this topic plus a full digital version of this book. Scan the QR code on page 31 or use your school's login at 12StoryLibrary.com.

Table of Contents

A Healthy Diet Prevents Many Diseases

For most of American history, children were rarely obese. But in the 1980s, eating habits started to change. People began eating more processed foods. These are foods that come in packages. They are often convenient and cheap. Today, one-third of American children are obese. What are the causes? One of them is processed foods. These foods are high in sugar, salt, and fat.

Obesity can lead to several health problems. These include high blood pressure and clogged blood vessels. Blood pressure is the force of blood surging through blood vessels. Eating too much salt causes the body to hold on to extra water. And this increases blood pressure, straining the heart. Eating unhealthy fats can increase levels of fat in blood. This blocks blood flow to the heart. And that can lead to a heart attack. Obesity can also weaken the immune system. The immune system fights infections

Fruits and vegetables are the best choices for a healthy diet.

Processed foods may be convenient, but most of them are unhealthy.

and cancers. With a weak immune system, a person has a higher risk of getting other diseases.

Fortunately, there's good news! A healthy diet can help prevent these diseases. The key is eating more fruits and vegetables. Whole grains are important, too. And it's always best to eat foods without added salt and sugar.

77

Percent of salt in a typical American's diet that comes from processed and restaurant food.

- Americans eat large amounts of sugar, salt, fats, and processed foods.
- This has contributed to obesity and related diseases.
- Children rarely had these diseases before the 1980s.
- A healthy diet can prevent diseases.

TV FOOD ADS AND OBESITY

The more TV a child watches, the more likely he or she is to become overweight. This is partly because the person is sitting and not exercising. It also happens because TV-watchers tend to snack on unhealthy foods. These are often the foods advertised on TV. In one study, researchers studied kids who watched shows with food commercials. These kids ate 45 percent more snack foods than kids who watched shows without food commercials.

Keep Tabs on Your Health

Heart disease is the number one killer in the United States. But most cases can be prevented. One way is to keep a healthy weight. Another way is to control high blood pressure and high cholesterol. These conditions often have no symptoms. That's why it's important to keep tabs on your health. For example, you should get regular blood pressure readings. Another good idea is to get a blood test for cholesterol and blood sugar.

A blood pressure test is a quick and easy way to keep tabs on your health.

One in three Americans has high blood pressure. Unfortunately, many do not know it. There are several ways to lower blood pressure. One way is to exercise regularly. Another way is to avoid smoking. Cutting back on salt also helps.

Cholesterol is fat in the blood. There are two types of cholesterol. One type is good, and one is bad. High levels of bad cholesterol can clog arteries. In time, this can lead to a heart attack. On the other hand, good cholesterol cleans out the bad cholesterol. There are ways to raise levels of good cholesterol. You can exercise. You can cut back on foods high in sugar and fat.

In people with diabetes, high blood sugar damages heart cells. It also increases the risk of diseases in several organs. The organs include the heart, kidneys, eyes, and those in the nervous system. There are ways to prevent these problems. You can control blood sugar through exercise and diet. Medications from the doctor can help, too.

80
Percent of people with type 2 diabetes who are overweight.

- Many people do not know they have high blood pressure.
- High blood pressure damages blood vessels and strains the heart.
- High cholesterol clogs blood vessels and can cause heart attacks.
- Uncontrolled diabetes damages many organs.
- It's important to monitor and control these conditions.

Simple Food Choices for Health

A healthy diet can help prevent illness. The foods you eat should include nutrients that provide energy. Your diet should also help the body grow and repair itself. There are different types of nutrients. They include proteins, fats, and carbohydrates. They also include vitamins and minerals.

Proteins are in meats and fish. They are in dairy products, too. They are also in nuts and beans. Proteins are important because they build cells and muscles.

Fats provide energy. They are also good for the brain. Fats in olive oil and some nuts are best for preventing disease. Small amounts of fats in meats and dairy are also healthy.

Carbohydrates, or carbs, are a type of sugar. The healthiest carbs are in fruits, vegetables, and whole

Salmon is full of vitamins, proteins, and healthy fats.

57.7
Percent of Americans who regularly eat fruits and vegetables.

- A healthy diet includes proteins, fats, and carbohydrates. It also includes vitamins and minerals.
- The healthiest carbs are in fruits, vegetables, and whole grains.
- The carbs in sugary foods contain few nutrients.
- Foods in their original form are healthiest.

THINK ABOUT IT

Many schools are serving healthier lunches. They are also banning soda machines. Has your school done this? What do you think of these changes?

grains. These foods contain many vitamins and minerals. They help fight disease, too. But other carbs have few nutrients and contribute to diseases. These carbs include the white sugar in foods such as doughnuts.

Foods in their original form are healthiest. This includes fruits and vegetables. They can be fresh or frozen. Other healthy choices include foods without added sugar and salt.

Frozen vegetables are both healthy and convenient.

9

Being Active Is Good for the Whole Body

Computers, TVs, and smartphones are great inventions. But in today's high-tech world, people are less active. Many kids spend about seven hours a day using electronic devices. Inactivity can lead to obesity and diseases. These diseases include heart disease, type 2 diabetes, and cancer.

Physical activity helps prevent these diseases. The activity does not have to be traditional exercise. For instance, you could walk or bike to school. You could walk a dog. You could go dancing. These are all healthy activities that don't seem like exercise.

In some activities, you use a lot of oxygen. These are called aerobic exercises. They include fast walking, jogging, and swimming. Aerobic activities strengthen the heart. They also lower blood sugar and blood pressure.

Other activities use less oxygen. These are called anaerobic exercises. They include short sprints

Kids and teens should do at least one hour of vigorous activity per day.

Aerobic exercises such as swimming improve blood flow and burn fat.

and lifting weights. This makes the body tougher and better able to fight disease. Both aerobic and anaerobic activities are important.

Consider making them part of your routine!

28

Percent of Americans ages 6 and older who are physically inactive.

- Many people are physically inactive in today's high-tech world.
- Inactivity contributes to obesity and many diseases.
- Physical activity helps prevent many diseases.
- Aerobic and anaerobic activities are important.

PHYSICAL ACTIVITY ENHANCES BOTH HEALTH AND FITNESS

Preventing disease requires both health and fitness. Physical activity enhances both. Health means the body parts work together the way they should. Fitness is the ability to do physical activity. An inactive lifestyle hurts health and fitness. It weakens all body parts, including the brain, bones, and muscles. It also weakens the heart and immune system.

Avoid Smoking

Each year, smoking kills more than 480,000 Americans. Smoking damages the entire body. Secondhand smoke is what people near a smoker breathe in. It is just as dangerous as smoking, especially to children. Yet 40 million Americans smoke. It's difficult to quit because cigarettes contain a drug called nicotine. Nicotine is addictive.

Cigarettes have hundreds of toxic chemicals. One of these chemicals is used in cleaning products. Another is used in rat poison.

And one is used in lighter fluid. More than 60 of the chemicals in cigarettes cause cancer. These chemicals also kill cells in the breathing tubes. That means body parts receive less oxygen than they need. This damages cells in the rest of the body.

Cigarette smoke also leads to heart disease. That's because the toxic chemicals cause blood vessels to swell. These chemicals raise blood pressure and cholesterol levels, too. They can also lead to diabetes.

The nicotine in cigarettes is addictive.

THINK ABOUT IT

Many places have banned smoking in public buildings. Yet millions of people smoke at home, even though they know about the dangers. Why do you think this is true?

People who stop smoking lower their risk for many diseases. The same is true for those who avoid secondhand smoke. Health experts say people who live with smokers should ask them not to smoke near others.

41,000
Number of Americans who die each year from secondhand smoke.

- Smoking is the largest preventable cause of disease and death in the United States.
- Smoking causes many diseases.
- Cigarettes contain hundreds of toxic chemicals that damage body parts.
- Avoiding smoking and secondhand smoke helps prevent illnesses.

Even if you don't smoke, it's unhealthy to be around someone who does.

Protect Yourself from Environmental Toxins

The environment contains human-made toxins. It contains natural toxins, too. Pesticides are human-made toxins. These sprays are put on crops and in homes. They kill insects and other pests. But some pesticides cause cancer. It's important to protect yourself from pesticides. Whenever possible, try to eat organic fruits and vegetables. They are grown without human-made pesticides.

Air pollution often leads to lung infections. This can happen indoors or outdoors. One cause is indoor wood-burning stoves. You can protect yourself by opening windows. This lets in fresh air. Air filters that remove dangerous particles can also help. Another cause is outdoor fumes from car exhaust. Try to stay indoors when outdoor air pollution levels are high. Do not run around if you must go outdoors.

It's a good idea to stay away from crops that are being sprayed with pesticides.

Car exhaust contributes to smog, a form of air pollution found in some cities.

Mold is another indoor toxin. It's best to have professionals test for and remove it. Mold grows in damp places with poor airflow. These places include bathrooms and basements. Mold can cause lung diseases and allergies. You can open windows and run fans in damp rooms to prevent mold.

4 million
Number of American families with children who are exposed to high levels of lead.

- Human-made and natural toxins in the environment cause diseases.
- These toxins are in polluted air, soil, and water.
- Radiation from the sun is another environmental hazard.
- Avoiding these environmental hazards can prevent disease.

Ultraviolet (UV) radiation from the sun is another environmental hazard. Cutting UV exposure helps prevent skin cancers. Use sunscreen lotion to block these rays. You can also wear a wide-brimmed hat and knit clothing.

THINK ABOUT IT

The sun's rays cause skin cancers. But many people think a suntan looks good. Do you think it's worth the risk?

Hand-Washing with Soap and Water Does Wonders

When you touch people or things, germs can get on your hands. Then, the germs can enter your body when you touch your mouth, eyes, or nose. Germs that cause colds and flu often spread this way.

How can you prevent diseases caused by germs? Hand-washing with soap and water is one of the best ways. There are certain times when it's especially important to wash hands. One is before eating or preparing food. Another is after sneezing or coughing. You should also wash your hands after using the toilet or handling garbage. It's also smart to wash your hands after touching an animal or shaking hands with someone.

Make sure you're washing your hands properly. First, get your hands wet. Next, apply soap. Then, rub your

Frequent hand-washing cuts the chances of getting a cold by about 20 percent.

hands together for at least 20 seconds. That's approximately how long it takes to sing "Happy Birthday" twice. Finally, rinse your hands and dry off with a clean towel. Sometimes soap and running water are not available. In that case, use a hand sanitizer that has at least 60 percent alcohol.

It's smart to wash your hands or use hand sanitizer after shaking hands with someone.

16

Percent by which respiratory infections can be reduced when people wash their hands.

- Hand-washing prevents diseases caused by germs.
- Germs that cause colds and flu often spread through touching.
- Always wash hands after touching objects, people, or animals.
- Proper hand-washing includes four steps.

REGULAR SOAP OR ANTIBACTERIAL SOAP?

Antibacterial soaps contain chemicals that kill bacteria. But they do not prevent illness better than regular soap does. Also, chemicals in antibacterial soaps make bacteria resistant to medications. Plus, these chemicals build up in water. Over time, this harms plants and animals in the environment. It's best to wash with regular soap and water.

17

Vaccines Are Powerful Anti-Disease Weapons

Vaccines are drugs that prevent many serious diseases. These diseases include polio, measles, whooping cough, and others. All these diseases are contagious. That means people can catch them from other people or animals. Many people died from these diseases before vaccines were invented.

Vaccines contain killed or weakened germs that cause these diseases. For instance, the measles vaccine contains weakened measles virus. It can't cause measles. It makes your immune system produce antibodies to the virus. Antibodies are chemicals that attack a specific germ. Someone with antibodies will not get sick if later exposed to the germ.

Most vaccines are given to babies and young children. Sometimes antibodies disappear over time. People then need booster vaccines to remain immune. It's important to receive vaccines and boosters even if a particular

Some vaccines are given as shots, while others are given by mouth or breathed in.

26

Number of known diseases that can be prevented with vaccines.

- Vaccines are drugs that prevent many serious diseases.
- Vaccines contain killed or weakened germs.
- Vaccines cause the recipient's immune system to produce antibodies.
- Antibodies prevent illness if the germ is encountered again.

illness is rare in your country. It may exist in other places, and travelers can bring it back with them.

THE VACCINE DEBATE

Studies show vaccines do more good than harm. Sometimes people have bad reactions to vaccines. Some parents claim vaccines killed their children or gave them autism. This has led to debates because some people refuse to vaccinate their children. Doctors believe unvaccinated people risk getting sick. They can then pass illnesses to those who cannot receive vaccines because of health issues. But those who oppose vaccines believe they have a right to choose which medications their children take.

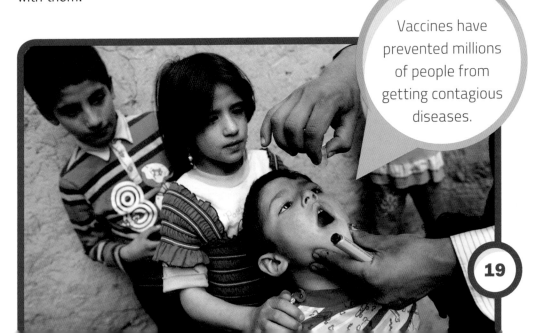

Vaccines have prevented millions of people from getting contagious diseases.

Sleep Helps Prevent Sickness

Do you get enough sleep? If you don't, you're increasing your risk for several diseases. These include type 2 diabetes, heart disease, and cancer. Lack of sleep makes the body release stress hormones. These hormones weaken the immune system and raise blood sugar. Lack of sleep can also cause weight gain. That's because the body increases levels of chemicals that make you hungry.

Doctors advise school-aged children to get nine to ten hours of sleep per night. Adults should get at least eight hours. There are several good ways to prepare for a good night's rest. You can avoid exercise, large meals,

Getting enough sleep helps your body produce more of the proteins that fight germs.

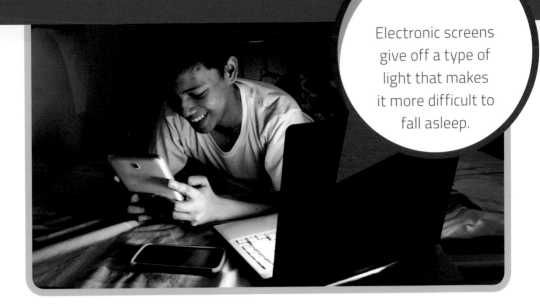

Electronic screens give off a type of light that makes it more difficult to fall asleep.

or caffeine before bedtime. Also, the bedroom should be cool, quiet, and dark. Another tip is to wind down for an hour. You can do calming activities like reading or taking a warm bath. It's not wise to use electronic devices before bedtime. Bright screens help keep people awake.

THE SLEEP-STRESS CONNECTION

Stress makes it difficult to sleep. Lack of sleep increases stress and promotes the release of stress hormones. This creates a cycle that can lead to many illnesses. Getting enough deep sleep can break this cycle. Deep sleep makes the brain tell the glands that produce stress hormones to stop doing so.

31
Percent of teens who get at least eight hours of sleep on an average school night.

- Lack of sleep increases the risk for many diseases.
- This disease risk occurs because a tired body produces stress hormones.
- Stress hormones weaken the immune system and have other bad effects.
- Getting enough sleep helps prevent these illnesses.

Watch Out for Disease-Spreading Insects and Animals

Each year, millions of people get diseases from bugs and other animals. Insects such as ticks and mosquitoes spread illnesses, including Lyme disease, malaria, and West Nile virus. They do this by biting people and animals. For instance, mosquitoes become infected with West Nile virus by biting a bird that carries the virus. The mosquito spreads the virus by biting a human or animal. This virus causes fever and headache. It can also cause brain swelling and sometimes death.

You can avoid insect bites by wearing long sleeves and long pants. Putting insect repellant on exposed skin also helps. You can spray it on shoes and clothing too.

Other animals, including pets, can also spread diseases. For example,

Always check for ticks after walking in the woods.

an infected cat can spread cat-scratch disease by scratching or biting a person. To prevent this, avoid rough play that makes a cat likely to scratch or bite.

Baby chicks and reptiles often carry bacteria in their waste. These bacteria cause stomach problems in people. Farm and petting zoo animals also carry many germs. It's important to wash hands well after touching any animal or cleaning its living space.

A mosquito net can prevent bites while you sleep.

1 million

Approximate number of people worldwide who die from insect-borne diseases each year.

- Insects spread many infectious diseases.
- Cover the skin with clothing or insect repellant to avoid insect bites.
- Animals, including pets, can also spread diseases to people.
- These diseases can be prevented with sanitary practices.

SMALL TURTLES DON'T MAKE GOOD PETS

Small turtles carry bacteria in their waste. The bacteria often get on whatever the turtles touch. In this way, the bacteria can spread to people. That's why it's illegal to sell small turtles as pets in the United States. Many people keep them anyway. In 2015, 51 people in the United States reported getting sick after touching small turtles.

23

Don't Let Your Food Make You Sick

Illness from contaminated food and water sickens up to 600 million people each year. Of these people, 420,000 die. The responsible germs are usually viruses and bacteria. They commonly cause vomiting and diarrhea. They can also cause kidney and liver disease. They can cause cancer as well.

Fortunately, there are ways to prevent illness from food. For example, you can avoid eating raw meat. You can also avoid raw fish and raw eggs. These foods are often contaminated. Also, be sure foods that need cooking are hot enough. For instance, ground meats such as hamburger should reach

A meat thermometer can help you make sure your food is properly cooked.

a temperature of at least 160° F (71° C). Poultry should reach 165° F (74° C). Do not eat meat or poultry that looks pink and undercooked.

Careful cleaning is another way to stay healthy. Be sure to clean anything that comes in contact with raw meat or eggs. That includes kitchen counters and cutting boards. It includes utensils and hands, too. It's also important to wash fresh fruits and vegetables before eating them. And be extra careful when traveling outside the United States. In many countries, it's safest to drink only bottled water. Avoid drinks with ice cubes, too.

48 million
Number of Americans who get sick from contaminated food each year.

- Contaminated food sickens hundreds of millions of people worldwide each year.
- The germs that cause these diseases commonly lead to vomiting and diarrhea.
- Avoiding undercooked foods helps prevent sickness.
- Cleaning raw produce and kitchen surfaces also helps.

Always wash fruits and vegetables with cold water before eating them.

Remember to Brush and Floss

Healthy teeth are good for overall health. Regular brushing and flossing helps prevent tooth decay and gum disease. Brushing and flossing can also prevent heart disease and lung disease. That's because those diseases may result from gum disease.

Gum disease happens when the gums become inflamed and infected. It results from plaque buildup on the teeth and gums. Plaque is a slimy, sticky mixture of bacteria, mucus, and food particles. Over time, the infection can destroy the gums and bones that hold teeth in place. Teeth may fall out or have to be removed.

Make sure you're not pressing too hard when you brush your teeth.

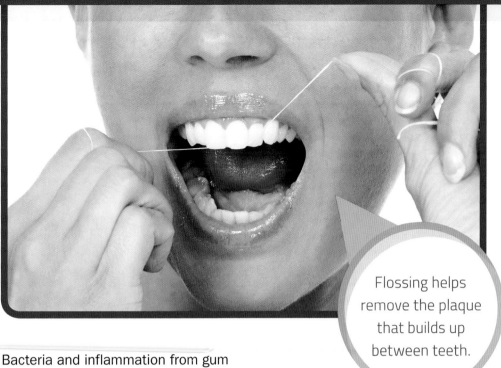

Flossing helps remove the plaque that builds up between teeth.

Bacteria and inflammation from gum disease can spread throughout the body. When this affects the heart, a heart attack or infection can result. If the infection spreads to the lungs, pneumonia is likely. Gum infections also increase the risk of Alzheimer's disease. This is a disease that affects memory and thought.

Dentists recommend brushing twice a day. They also recommend flossing once a day. If you do these things, you will have healthy teeth. And that will help prevent tooth decay and gum disease. It's best to visit a dentist every six months for a checkup and teeth cleaning. Another way to keep your teeth healthy is avoiding sugary foods and drinks.

120
Number of seconds you should spend brushing your teeth.

- Gum disease results from plaque buildup on the teeth and gums.
- Bacteria and swelling from gum disease can spread throughout the body.
- Good oral hygiene helps prevent tooth decay and gum disease.
- It also helps prevent illnesses linked to gum disease.

Fact Sheet

- Organizations such as the American Academy of Pediatrics advise limiting kids' total screen time to less than two hours per day. This includes TV, video games, smartphones, and tablets.

- People who watch more than two hours of TV per day have a greatly increased risk of type 2 diabetes, heart disease, and early death.

- Many people are surprised that certain processed foods contain so much salt. A corn dog contains 350 to 620 milligrams. One ounce of potato chips has 50 to 200 milligrams. Doctors recommend that most people should eat less than 2,300 milligrams of salt per day. Most Americans eat approximately 3,500 milligrams per day.

- On average, Americans consume 31 percent more calories, 56 percent more fats, and 14 percent more sugars than they did in the 1970s. This is mostly because of processed and fast foods.

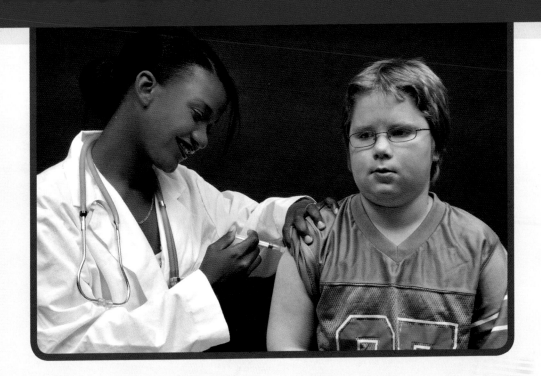

- Besides containing healthy vitamins and minerals, plant-based foods also contain nutrients called phytonutrients. These nutrients are known to prevent many diseases such as heart disease and cancer.

- Physical and mental stress increase the risk of physical and mental illnesses. Doctors recommend doing relaxing things such as listening to music, doing yoga, or hanging out with good friends to decrease stress.

- Besides frequent hand-washing, there are other ways to prevent contagious diseases. They include staying away from people who are sick and not touching your mouth, nose, and eyes after touching anyone or anything that may contain germs.

- The skin cancers that can result from exposure to UV rays often do not appear for many years after sunburns occurred. To prevent this damage, wear sunscreen and re-apply every two hours. Stay out of the sun in the late morning and early afternoon, when rays are strongest.

29

Glossary

addictive
Causing a person to want something and be unable to stop using it.

antibody
A chemical that attacks and kills a specific germ.

bacteria
A type of germ that can cause illness.

contagious
Able to spread from one person or animal to another.

inflammation
Redness and swelling.

obese
Having too much body fat.

overweight
Having too much weight for a particular height.

pesticide
A chemical that kills pests such as insects.

toxin
A poison.

vaccine
A medicine that prevents illness.

virus
A type of germ that can cause illness.

For More Information

Books

Blattner, Don, and Blattner Howerton, Lisa. *Health, Wellness, and Physical Fitness, Grades 5–8.* Greensboro, NC: Mark Twain Media, 2013.

Gray, Shirley Wimbish. *Prevention and Good Health.* North Mankato, MN: The Child's World, 2014.

Sjonger, Rebecca. *How to Choose Foods Your Body Will Use.* New York: Crabtree, 2016.

Visit 12StoryLibrary.com

Scan the code or use your school's login at **12StoryLibrary.com** for recent updates about this topic and a full digital version of this book. Enjoy free access to:

- Digital ebook
- Breaking news updates
- Live content feeds
- Videos, interactive maps, and graphics
- Additional web resources

Note to educators: Visit 12StoryLibrary.com/register to sign up for free premium website access. Enjoy live content plus a full digital version of every 12-Story Library book you own for every student at your school.

Index

About the Author

Melissa Abramovitz is an award-winning freelance writer and author who specializes in writing educational nonfiction books and magazine articles for all age groups, from preschoolers through adults.

READ MORE FROM 12-STORY LIBRARY

Every 12-Story Library book is available in many formats. For more information, visit 12StoryLibrary.com.